PUPPY KISSES

NANETTE M. DAY

INKWELL INTERNATIONAL

So mom packed us all up in the car—Lily, my big sister of a black lab who thinks she's top dawg (despite being a little deaf); Charlie the marshmallow cat and my best bud; Jack the peacemaker cat; Baby the calico cat, whose giant attitude makes up for her tiny size; and me, pittie pup extraordinaire—and we headed out for a new adventure, ending up in the middle of nowhere! We now officially live in the country! Our nearest human neighbor is a mile away, but we've got all sorts of exciting non-human neighbors, like deer and bunnies and hawks and pheasants and oodles of birds, which the cats find entertaining but me? Meh. And the best part? The fields of grass that stretch above my head and I get to run through in search of adventure. Every time I go outside, it feels like I am going on a safari in the wilds of Africa. Who knew Nebraska could be so fun!

2

Hmm, so mom is not letting me run outside 24/7, no matter how much I whine and give her my super sweet "pretty please" eyes. What's the point of being in the country if I can't run outside all the time?! Plus, how rude is it that I am not going out to greet all out new neighbors who keep stopping by to meet us? There are several deer meandering through the trees and fireflies are dancing among the flowers, but here I sit, perched at the window, just watching.

I should really call the ASPCA and let them know of the abuse going on here.

3

I can't sleep. I am too excited about all the fun waiting to be had outside while I am stuck inside. Where is the sun? Come out and play, Mr. Sun, so I can too!

The fireflies are still playing. Even while the moon shines through the trees, the fireflies play.

Clearly their mom loves them.

4

A giant spider came to visit, crawling up the wall. I snuffled it and said howdy, but he wasn't too friendly. Then again, with mom screaming like she was, I wouldn't have been too friendly either.

I don't know why she gets all upset by spiders. Baby always gets them anyway, always chewing off their legs (like she did this one). She's weird that way.

I hope she never decides to chew off my legs...

Oh, the humiliation! I can't believe I have to wear this stupid piece of round plastic around my head!!!

Mom took me for a ride and I was SO EXCITED but then we ended up at the v-e-t. Ugh! And as if that wasn't bad enough, they sent me home with this stupid cone thingee. Now I'm kinda glad that mom didn't let me meet all the neighbors yet. How embarrassing to have to explain this cone to them.

The only good news is that Baby is scared of the cone, so at least my legs should be safe for the next 10 days.

6

Cone of shame 0, Pistachio 1.

I am the victor! It only took me six days, but I got the entire cone torn off. I went to show mom my feat, but she was not as impressed. I don't understand humans sometimes.

Mom! Mom! Mom! Look!

Two squirrels. By the leaves. See them? No, not there... over there! Yes, there! That pile of leaves—can you see them playing hide and seek?

Can I go play too? Pleeeeeeasssse?! I promise to be a good boy and not hurt my new friends. Oh—and look! A third one has joined in the fun.

I promise to be a good boy if you let me have some fun with the squirrels. Just this once...

War is imminent.

The stinky Asian lady beetles are facing off against the silly house flies. Both sides are building giant armies for the ultimate onslaught.

The growing herd of squirrels (still!) playing in leaves in the yard are rooting for the flies. The bouquet of pheasants in the brush are cheering on the beetles.

Everyone gets to have fun except me. It's so not fair.

I found a new friend, but I'm not sure what it is. It is trapped in the wall behind the shower. I can hear it climbing up the wall, then sliding back down. It keeps doing it over and over. (I never said it was a smart friend.) It sounds bigger than Baby's head, but I'm sure I could still pick it up with my mouth.

Hmm, I wonder what it is?

My new friend is gone, hunted down by them darn kitties. Mom keeps praising them giving them catnip (which makes Baby's eyes huge ... she scares me when she's on the mint). I didn't even get to say hello to my new friend before mom helped him go outside (and she wouldn't let me go outside and meet him!). Mom called him a vole.

I'm gonna have to see if I can find another one of these voles and say howdy.

Hundreds of birds are performing a ballet swarm right outside my window perch. I'm not too fond of birds. They're not bad friends, but they are always flying so I can never say howdy to them. Not very friendly, if you ask me. But now they're giving me my own personal show, which is kind of pretty.

Unless they're trying to warn me about something...?

Oh yummy! Nom nom nom.

Mom is making dinner and it smelled so yummy I had to go let her know, but she was busy in the other room so I just gave the pan a quick inspection. You know, to make sure nothing was burning or anything (because mom burns a lot of food!). And I sniffed and no burning smells, but such a yummy smell that I just had to taste what she was making. Maybe she was making it for me? It was so yummy! Yes, she must have been making it for me. At least a little bit. She would share with me. So I cleaned my half of the pan for her. You know, to save her the trouble.

Now she's staring down at me, frowning. I don't understand. I did good! I cleaned up the pan. But she's saying the curry was not mine to eat. Why not?

Maybe if I sit all nice and give her the "where's my treat?" look she'll give me a little more. A pup can dream.

13

I just found a new friend! I was walking past the new furniture mom got delivered and saw him watching me. A handsome fella, but he startled me at first, so I growled at him. He growled back, so I naturally barked. He barked back! So I raced over to say hello, and then mom told me to stop getting her mirror dirty with all my nose prints.

14

The white stuff has returned!

Mom took us outside to play this morning and *brrr* it was cold, especially my paws. She let us loose to run but I didn't want to go anywhere but back inside because it was so gosh-darn cold. Crazy Lily just went around eating up all the white stuff on the ground. I sniffed it, but it didn't smell special (and certainly not as yummy as mom's curry), so I left it for Lily to eat. Not that she could eat up all the white stuff on the ground because it was *everywhere*. But she tried!

And then mom scooped up some of that cold white stuff and made it into a ball and threw it at me. Oh, snowballs! I love chasing snowballs! Yay, winter has returned!

15

There's a group of pheasants walking past the kitchen window. I keep telling mom, but she just tells me to be quiet. I want to go say hello! Not being able to go out and play with the new neighbors ... this is puppy hell, isn't it? I'm just gonna sit here and whine until mom lets me go outside.

M om finally let us go outside again. Of course, the pheasants were all gone by then. It's like she doesn't want me to be all neighborly—I don't understand!

While we were out exploring all the snow Lily found a full-grown vole. She's so lucky! She took it back to mom to show off, but mom made her drop it. I sniffed it a few times, but it wasn't moving. Mom said it was frozen. Poor little vole.

Then the shadow passed overhead and we all looked up. Mom corralled us back inside, saying we had interrupted the young hawk's lunch date.

Lily may be mostly deaf and somewhat blind, but she can sure find some fun. We were outside, exploring the new homestead when she discovered a group of new friends: wild turkeys. The turkeys were startled and gobbled. Lily was startled and ran away. Mom and I laughed.

Another new friend. Can you believe all the friends out here in the country? Such a fun place!

This new friend is sitting outside the back door and howling—yes, howling!—for us to come out and play. I keep jumping up and begging mom to let me go say hi, but she's is being really determined tonight and saying no way Jose. She called this friend a coyote and said he's probably not alone.

Not alone?! Then let's welcome in the whole band of coyotes in and maybe give them some of that yummy curry to warm them up from the cold!

Nope, not happening. Mom is being adamant. Probably a good thing, I guess. The cats wouldn't be so welcoming and friendly, anyway, seeing as they are busy preparing for the apocalypse while the coyote keeps howling.

Mr. Coyote is back! He has returned for an encore performance of howling at the very low-hanging, quite rotund moon. I tried to sing with him, but mom said that was rude because I was interrupting him and all, so I sang quietly to myself (mom calls that whining).

W e have new friends! We have new friends! And they're the bestest new friends a pupper could dream of!

They're big and black and stand right along the dog run, chewing on the grass and sometimes mooing at us and I just wanna run out and nip at their heels to say "hello, friend!"

And then I see more coming over to stare at us and I jump-run-happy-nark-dance some more because cows! How cool is that? I told mom we absolutely must invite them over for dinner some time, but she poo-pooed that idea super quick. No fun! But cows! We have cows!

They stay in the cornfields along the edges of where I can run, so I can't ever go greet them properly, but I make sure to bark a "hello howdy how are you" greeting to each and every one of them so they know I am being the friendliest of new friends.

21

I really gotta pee but it's so *brrr* outside! Mom opened the door and told us to "go run," but both and Lily ran back into the house instead.

How many days until summer?

22

I feel that it is my civic duty to let anybody who is wondering know the proper dog etiquette after running around outside in the muddy environs. It's quite straightforward actually. After getting as muddy as possible, race into the bedroom and roll around on the bed until all the mud has been wiped off the paws.

Of course, you might want to give the cats who are sleeping on the bed a heads up before you cover them in mud. (I Charlie the marshmallow doesn't stay mad at me for too long.)

M om took us out for an early morning run, but when we got outside ... it was spooky!

The acreage was enshrouded in fog. Everything was very still. Deathly still. Send-shivers-down-my-spine still. (I had to shake it off just thinking about it.)

Halfway to the dog run, an owl sounded off in the barn. Both me and Lily freeze, afraid to move and scare away the interloper. Mom kept prodding us to move, but I really wanted to go check out that sound (I've never seen an owl up close and personal before, and now was our chance...).

We finally started moving again, but I kept glancing back toward that sound. I never did get to see the owl, which made me sad.

Until we got to the dog run and I forgot all about the owl because I heard something moving through the fields surrounding the run. The super tall grasses were moving in all directions, but there wasn't any wind. So I started running back and forth, barking and howling at whatever visitor was in the grass (because, you know, I wanted to be all polite and welcome it to our home). Mom wasn't too thrilled about that because my barking made the moving grass come closer to us.

She made us do our thing as quickly as possible and then dragged us back toward the house. I kept looking over my shoulder and barking at the visitor to come with us, but mom kept pulling us forward.

And then something ran through the trees on the other side of the house. It was big and it was fast and mom froze, telling us we were trapped between whatever is moving in the grasses behind us and whatever was racing back and forth in the trees in front of us. Trapped? I told her we weren't trapped—we were popular!

She frantically pulled us inside while mumbling that she didn't want to have to chase us in this crazy deathly stillness surrounded by preternatural beings if we got loose.

We finally get inside the house, where mom says it's "safe," and Baby jumps down from a cabinet, startling mom and making her scream.

I laughed at that, but I hid it from mom because she was clearly spooked. I curled up with her on the couch so we could watch some movies and put my head on her lap so she knew I was protecting her.

It was dusk before mom took us out for a walk again, but she was still having trouble shaking that creep-vibe she got from the morning walk. She kept pointing out how the barren tree limbs seemed poised to pluck us from our surroundings and take us to unknown worlds and how the shadows hid the worst monsters of our imaginations.

I'll be honest, she was kinda creeping me out with all her spooky comments.

But then again, maybe she knows something about trees plucking and monsters hiding because we discovered that the dead vole that Lily had brought to show off a while back (and to whom mom gave a proper burial when the hawk decided it's lunch companion was no longer delectable) had been ripped from its earthly grave!

Mom clearly knew something weird was afoot.

Luckily, tonight, there is no fog, just a big, beautiful creamy moon (as mom would say: cue the werewolves).

C'mon, mom. Time to wake up. Up up up. Move it. Up and at'em. Time to make the doughnuts (or better yet, dog treats).

There ya go. That's it. Right up on out of bed...

...so I can snuggle back into your spot for a few more hours of uninterrupted snoring.

Yesterday the snow was super deep—almost up to my belly—which made running through it super fun. Nothing can beat a good snow run!

Oh, except when the snow melts enough to just cover my paws, which made me super bummed at first when we went outside today, but then mom said it was the perfect consistency for playing snowball fetch. She was so right! I bet I caught a million gazillion snowballs!!!

I didn't want to stop chasing them, but mom got tired, so we came back inside. I gotta say, all this snuggly warmth after chasing the snowballs is making me so tired ... *yawn*

snore snore snore

Y awn
I feel bad for the kitties because they don't get to chase snowballs. All they do is sleeping in the sunny, warm window all day long.

yawn

I think I should join them ... (such smart kitties!)

Bow wow!
I can't stop laughing because mom is such a funny lady.

She went to call Lily inside, but Lily was out front and ignoring mom. So mom walked around the porch until Lily noticed her and came running. But then as she tried to get up the steps, poor Lily's back legs gave out. I was really worried because Lily is pretty old, but mom was out there (I was inside the front door watching everything).

Mom walked down the steps to help Lily up from behind—at least, I think that is what she was trying to do. Unfortunately, the steps were a solid sheet of ice. Mom ended up doing a split on the steps, pinning leg underneath her. She was still in her pjs, so she was giving all the neighbors quite a show.

I know, I know, I shouldn't be laughing, but it really was funny looking.

She finally managed to get up and help Lily, who fell down the steps sideways. Then they decided go to the back door (no steps!) to get back inside. Whew!

Everyone is finally safe and sound (although the squirrels were still giggling about getting the full show).

I am soooo tired. I went running in the snow again. So.
Much. Fun. But now ... tired. Trying not to fall asleep.
Must keep watch. But my eyes are heavy ... heavy ...
heavy ...

    snoooooore

A very healthy mouse just ran by all three cats and both of us dogs. I figured the cats would get mad if I tried to catch the mouse (they get first dibs), so I didn't do anything. But Lily, who likes to gobble up everything (mom calls her a mobile garbage disposal) didn't snap up the mouse either. We all just watched as it ran back and forth, trying to avoid mom, who was screaming loud enough to rattle the windows.

Must be Monday.

Jack Jack kitty cat has a sneezy wheezy cold.
Charlie the marshmallow has a sore paw.
Me? I have a need to run wild ...

I t's that time again: time for a new neighbor. Today's addition is what mom calls woodpeckers. Personally, I call them crazy. They just go around banging their faces on all the trees (and I do mean *all* the trees). Why would someone do that? It doesn't sound like very much fun, and I think the squirrels are probably not too happy at all about all that noise rattling their homes.

It is such a crazy noise too. Mom calls it incessant. It's kinda giving me a headache. Poor squirrels. It must be really bad for them. If I could fly, I would chase away all those woodpeckers and their loud *rat-a-tat-tat rat-a-tat-tat rat-a-tat-tat*.

The crazy thing is the cats just continue to sleep, oblivious to it all. Silly cats.

33

I probably shouldn't tell you what I witnessed this morning, because I think Charlie the marshmallow cat will lose his cat license if I do. So promise not to tell anyone else, okay? Deal?

Mom has a place where she feeds the cats in the kitchen (a place where we dogs can't get to, which is frustrating because I really like cat food ... oh, wait, this is Charlie's story). Okay, so the place where she feeds the cats is next to a window, and outside the window is a little bush that attracts birds. Charlie was sitting by the window, waiting for his breakfast, when he pressed his nose to the window.

A little itty-bitty bird flew up and landed on the bush right next to Charlie (on the other side of the glass, of course). Charlie perked up. The birdie jumped closer to Charlie. Charlie swished his tail. The birdie jumped even closer. Charlie let loose an "I'm-gonna-get-you-birdie" cater-waul. The birdie bobbed its head at the window, clearly signaling "friend!"

Charlie jerked back, turned, and ran to hide ... under the bed in another room!

Cats around the world are bowing their heads in shame.

34

Oh those crazy woodpeckers! Now they have discovered the (metal) grain bins. They were having a total jam session this morning, which was giving everyone a headache.

But then their music drew the attention of a hawk that circled several times before settling on a tree branch (front row seats!). After that, the woodpeckers' music seemed to lack a certain confidence they had before

(Btw, the squirrels are still furious about the disruptions. They have been picketing protest, walking up and down the driveway all day.)

35

Mom really knows how to take the fun out of a great day.

We spent several hours outside today. Mom was working on the homestead. She played tag with a garter snake (she let him get away). Lily played tag with a mouse (the mouse lost). I played tag with a rotting corpse of something in the weeds. I thought we all won on that one but it turns out I lost.

One intense bath later and I am all squeaky clean. Mom ruins all my fun!

36

Mr. Spider thinks he is being all sneaky racing across the wall before anyone sees him. But I see him. I see everything.

Don't worry, Mr. Spider. I won't tell Baby what you're doing. As long as you stay up there, she will not be able to chew your legs off. Just do me a favor while you're up there and feast on all those stinky Asian beetles that think they own my home. Bon appetit!

The poor kitties never get to go outside and enjoy the wonders of the world beyond the front door (like the squirrels and the snowballs and the rotting corpses). I always feel so sad for them.

But today I realized they don't need to look beyond the front door because a family of barn swallows built a nest about the door on the porch. The cats are loving the live entertainment, which means I get the best of all the snuggly sleeping spots all to myself.

38

The skies are making all sorts of noises. It's not the boom-boom sound that rattles the windows and makes Lily nervous, but more like a rumbly grumbly sound that travels from one side of the world to the other. It doesn't seem to bother Lily at all, but just between you and me, it's making it too difficult for me to sleep.

Mom went outside to look around and I watched her from the big picture window, ready to warn her if anything tried to sneak up behind her. The squirrels and birds were following her around the property. They were obviously freaked out too. But mom didn't stay outside long, especially after something in the weeds started rustling around and following her.

When she came back inside, I offered to go out and check on the rustling for her, but for once I am perfectly happy that she said no. I think it'll just be better for me to stay snuggled up with mom until the rumbling skies quiet down.

39

I woke mom up to let her know that a gang of about 15 turkeys were running full throttle down the middle of the road. Mom told me to go back to bed.

Now I am sitting on the TV stand (I pushed the TV to the floor so I could fit my whole butt on the stand) and watching the turkeys race.

You know I could outrun them all. I would so totally win that race!

40

Pistachio: Mom! Mom! Mom! Look! Mom! Look! Look! Out there! Outside! Look! Look! Now! Mom! Now! Now!

Mom: Okay, okay, Pistachio. You don't need to bark so much.

Pistachio: But, mom! Mom! Mom! Look! Outside! Look! Do you see it? Do you see the aliens invading? I will protect you, mom! I promise! Just let me get them and I will protect you!

Mom: It's just the farmers driving their giant tractors to the fields.

Pistachio: Aliens! They're aliens, mom! They're here to invade! I'll protect you, mom! Mom! Mom! See? I'll protect you! Promise!

Mom: It's okay, P-dawg. Just calm–

Pistachio: Mom! Mom! Mom! Look! Turkeys! The turkeys are running away from the aliens, mom! Save the turkeys! Run, turkeys, run!

Turkeys: Crap crap crap crap crap crap crap crap crap ...

Pistachio: Save the turkeys! Run, turkeys, run!

Turkeys: Crap crap crap crap crap crap crap crap crap ...

Pistachio: Mom! Mom! Save the turkeys! Run! Run! Run!

Mom: Where did I put that bottle of migraine meds?

41

I think Mr. Spider has decided that we are friends now. He follows me from room to room. I go to sleep and he's on the wall. I wake up and he's on the wall. I go out to pee and when I return, he's waiting for me. He must have a bad case of separation anxiety.

I hope Baby doesn't think we are in cahoots. I don't want her chewing on my legs.

Third day without dog treats. Lily and I met with the cats to discuss the situation. Revolution is imminent.

43

Mom said the rumbling skies are coming back. She said it's gonna rain good this time, but hopefully the rumblies won't come too close to use. Paws crossed.

I asked her if we should share the news with the squirrels and turkeys and (ugh!) woodpeckers, but she said they are all already hunkered down and ready to wait out the storm.

I still have my doubts. If it's gonna be as bad as she said, don't you think we should bring everybody inside, where it's safe?

44

The turkeys survived the storm! The turkeys survived the storm! I woke up this morning and they were on the front porch, just waiting to say hello. (I told you we should have let everyone inside!)

I barked "good morning, friends!" to them, but I must have startled them because they took off running in all directions. So I ran to the picture window to look for them. Then I ran to the kitchen window. Finally I ran upstairs and checked the window by the stairs and then all the bedroom windows.

They were running into the trees to hide. Sad. They must not like morning puppy breath.

45

I woke up from my afternoon nap to see the turkeys hanging out on my grass by the picture window, so of course I plastered my face to the window pane to say howdy. The turkeys shot across the road and then settled into the field, but I could still hear them singing *neener* to me.

Mom wouldn't let me out to play no matter how high pitched I made my whiney barking.

Turkeys have all the fun.

46

S O NOT FAIR

I begged mom to let me go outside, but she took one look through the window and said no way.

So now I am stuck inside, my nose rammed into the window to I can watch two squirrels playing tag with the wild turkeys.

So far, it is squirrels 1, turkeys 0.

(One turkey high-tailed it into the neighboring field.)

This game would be a BILLION times more fun if I could just get outside and join the fun.

47

W e have deer!

Oh, they're so pretty and big and healthy and friendly in their aloof sort of way (I speak fluent deer, just in case you were wondering).

I was outside for my morning constitutional, leg raised to just the right height, when a deer walked around the corner and stared at me. He was only a few leaps and bounds away from me, but I kept my cool (and kept my leg raised, as that is the polite thing to do in such circumstances). We stared at each other for several (racing) heartbeats before he turned and ran.

My heart is still racing. I really wanted to go frolic with him, but you can probably guess what mom said about that idea.

So cool to see a deer all up close like that. I will just have to frolic with him in my dreams.

48

I was keeping watch over the turkeys as they explored the fields (of course, I had to keep watch from the picture window, which really isn't ideal, but mom just will not listen to me no matter how hard I try to convince her).

Everything was peaceful outside, but then a pheasant decided to make a house call on the turkeys and introduce himself. I begged mom to let me go introduce myself as well (it's only polite, after all!). Anybody wanna take a wild guess at her reaction?

Harrumph.

49

A moment of silence for one of the little female turkeys.

I sniffed out the crime scene and, best I can tell, she tried to escape something by running/flying into the garage door. Sadly, she broke her neck.

It's kinda creepy when you realize that whatever scared her didn't stop to pick her up. That doesn't seem right to me. I brought her to mom, and we had a burial for her.

Rest in peace, lady turkey.

50

We spent the afternoon outside today so mom could mow down some of the grass. She tied me up to a tree by my water dish and pool, which was fine by me because it was hot out there! Although, if I had my way, I would be on the riding lawn mower with here, because that is the best spot for me. I tried to convince her of that today, but she wasn't listening.

Maybe she will now.

She just got chased off the riding lawn mower by a freakishly large turkey (his head reached mom's shoulder while she was on the mower). He charged her on the mower so powerfully that she had to scramble off the machine because it wouldn't turn fast enough for her to get away. I think he was the same turkey pacing in front of the garage earlier this afternoon (where the other turkey died). He seemed to calm down when the mower sputtered off.

Mom said she was done mowing for the day. Next time, she really should take me as her co-pilot.

The turkeys are having quite the party this afternoon. I wasn't invited. This is what happens when you don't get to be neighborly with people.

(Mom says it's my "overexuberance," whatever that means.)

Mom said whispers of a revolution among the area wildlife are afoot. Not sure what that means, but apparently the local wildlife leaders are upset about us domesticated furries.

It all started when Lily was spotted running from the barn, with three extremely agitated turkeys in pursuit. Mom was able to calm everyone down from that episode, but then I decided to play tag with a snake (my first ever snake friend), which seemed to fuel the fires. Mom was not happy about trying to separate me from the snake (or the snake from me).

Everyone is safe ... for now. But we are surrounded, and mom's caffeine supplies are dwindling. Don't know how much longer we can last ...

53

Mom has decided that I have something called ESP because I was sleeping (she said "conked out and snoring away!) when I suddenly jumped up and ran clear across the house to a new window, where I started barking.

I tried to explain to her that it wasn't ESP or even really good hearing. It's just that those rascally rabbits are super loud chewers when they munch of the grass. They're so loud they woke me up from my nap!

Admit it, you'd be barking at them too.

Pistachio: OMG OMG OMG OMG OMG OMG OMG OMG OMG OMG OMG OMG OMG OMG OMG OMG OMG OMG OMG OMG OMG OMG OMG OMG OMG OMG OMG OMG OMG OMG OMG OMG OMG OMG OMG OMG OMG OMG OMG OMG OMG OMG OMG OMG OMG OMG OMG OMG!

Mom: What's up, buddy?

Pistachio: TRACTOR!!

The dandelions are in attack mode.

I went outside for my morning roll in the grass and came back inside with a yellow coat. The cats laughed at me. They said it looks like I peed on myself.

I tried to rub the yellow off on the carpet, but mom yelled at me, so now I am moping in my kennel, dreaming about the next time mom decides to mow.

I'll get even with those dandelions one way or another.

56

A pheasant just strutted across the front yard.

Now mom's been trying to tell me that I shouldn't get so overexcited when I meet new friends, and I was remembering how all the turkeys ran away from me the last time I checked on them, so this time I decided to play it cool.

Well, I tried to.

I wasn't sure whether to bark in excitement or warning, so I ended up sitting at the door and whining between half barks.

The pheasant just continued on his nonchalant little way, which wasn't very friendly behavior, if you ask me. But he didn't run away from me either, so I am going to mark this one up as a win.

Pistachio 1, new neighbors ... oh what the heck—we're all winners!

The birds are awfully chatty this evening. Wonder what they know that we don't ... ?

Okay, like I said, me and birds? Not the closest of friends. Oh, sure, I am best buds with the turkeys and (hopefully soon) the pheasant, but those little flitty birds that hang out in the trees all day? Well, we just don't get to say howdy to each other too often.

But today ... oh, today!

A little birdy just flew up to the picture window, where Jack was sitting and enjoying the morning sun. Naturally Jack reached up with front paws to nab this new friend (because cats really do not understand that whole "be neighborly" thing) and promptly fell backward off the table.

I was trying to hold in my snort-giggling as Jack stood up and sauntered into the kitchen, giving everyone the whole "it's cool, I meant to do that" look.

Today is an epic day that will go down in the history books, for on this day, at some time during the night (mom yelled that it was 3 a.m.) I discovered the Sacred Meeting of the Bunnies.

The world shall never be the same.

Butterflies ... butterflies everywhere!
And female pheasants racing through the grass while a bluebird watches.
Even the squirrels seem happier today.
Man, those bunnies ... they gots da power!

Oh holy moly, mom—turn it off!

I am trying to sleep here. I need my afternoon naps or I won't have the energy to chase the monsters from the trees all night.

I don't care if that alarm thing that keeps going off every fifteen minutes is telling you about more bad weather headed our way. I need to sleep!

62

There is a phenomenon in Nebraska that occurs when the sun is on its way to new places and the opposite horizon is the deep periwinkle blue of distant storms: At this precise moment, the greens of the trees and grass, set against the earthy yellows of the freshly plowed fields and that haunting periwinkle, become an intensely rich organic green not seen anywhere else. And as if the whole world knows the magic of this very moment, the birds become calm, the butterflies come to rest, and even the wind slows to silence, all taking the rare opportunity to enjoy the quiet intensity.

Of course, I am color-blind, so I'm just staring out the window waiting for the nighttime neighbors to emerge from their hiding places.

63

Mom went outside to take pictures of the full moon and got mauled by bunnies. I tried to warn her, but she never listens to me. Bunnies have special powers at night.

64

Sitting sentry at my window, watching an acreage shrouded in dust. It's dark out, but the farmer is still working in the fields, driving his tractor back and forth in front of my window.

Mom keeps telling me that everything is okay, that the farmer is just doing his job, but I know better. Those lighting patterns on his tractor? Those are signals to the bunnies.

The bunnies are preparing their invasion.

65

A gang of goldfinches has muscled their way onto the acreage, and as much as I am *meh* about little flitty birds ... well, these gangster-wannabes just need to move on.

The robins are not thrilled by the interlopers. They keep marching in protest back and forth across the front lawn. Even the squirrels are getting in on the action.

I feel like I should be out there, with them. If not to chase off the goldfinches, then at least to march in solidarity with my squirrel buddies.

66

Mom! Mom! Mom! I found baby bunnies! Here. I brought one to you. Unfortunately it's an orphan ow because Lily (the garbage disposal) found the other one. Lemme go see if any others are there.

...

Moooooooooooooooooooooooooooooommm!

I found the mama bunny. Lemme catch her for you.

I can get her, really. And then we can reunite the family.

Oh, she's a sly one, dodging left and right, but I will get her!

Uh, she seems to be on speed.

She might run faster than even me! How is that possible?

I'll get her over her. No, over there.

Finally! I caught her, mom. And she's such a good play friend, I'm gonna play with her some more. We're gonna roll in the grass together, 'kay?

Mom? She's not moving. Is she napping? It's not time for afternoon naps, mom. Wake her up, please.

Aw, what do you mean it's time to go inside? What about my new friends? Are you sure they'll be okay out here without us? Maybe we should build a little cubby for them inside. Charlie will share his nap cubby, won't he?

Bye-bye bunny friends!

Lily just brought back the remnants of a male turkey (mostly just feathers). She was so proud of her find and excited to show it off to mom. She wouldn't share it with me, of course.

She was pretty disappointed when mom wouldn't let her in the house with her treasure.

C *ough cough.*

Um, mom, can you turn on the air-conditioner outside, please? That fiery wind is burning my lungs every time I breathe, which makes it really hard to run and romp and play. Never mind the gritty sand that is ripping at my skin! Oh, and I saw migrating dust devils that threatened to whisk me away ...

Why isn't that weather alarm thingee sounding off now? Oops, that right. I forgot I ate it. Sorry.

ough cough.

Okay, mom, I think you left the air-conditioner on outside too long and something broke and now it is like I am trying to breathe under a blanket of water!

If I wanted to feel this wet, I'd just go swimming in my pool.

70

All right, this isn't funny anymore. If I can't go outside to play with all the neighbors, then they can't come taunt me at the picture window.

Three rabbits, two squirrels, and I won't even count all the various birds hanging out right in front of the picture window—so close I could pounce them in a single jump. Yeah, you go look for your migraine meds, mom, because I am just gonna sit here barking all day until I can join in the fun.

hy? Why is everyone being so mean to me? What did I do to deserve such mean friends?

The bunnies are playing Ring around the Rosie with the evergreen trees. Do you know how good I am at that game? I am the bestest! But you won't let me out to play with them.

And the squirrels! The squirrels are running around your car in circles. It started with just two squirrels, but now there are five of them out there, running round and round and round, as fast as they can go. You know I could run just as fast as them!

Plus there's a hawk circling overhead. I bet he wants to join in the fun too. Yup, there he goes, diving in ...

Oh, wait ...

Hey! That's not how you play that game!

72

Mom! Mom! Mom! There's a flying thing, a bird, outside, trying to find shelter from the wind. It keeps flying into the window, smacking its head against the glass. What do I do? What do I do?

Oh my gosh. There it goes again! Stop, little birdy! Don't worry. Mom will open up the door and you can fly straight inside, right mom?

Mom? What do you mean "this isn't a bird sanctuary"? C'mon, mom, Pleeeeaaassse??!

73

M om's been grumbling at me all night, but I swear it wasn't my fault!

She took us out to run at dusk, right before a powerful storm was moving in quickly—and you know the storms up here make all the wildlife go a little nutso, so she shouldn't have been surprised that I happened to interrupt five bunnies having a mini conference right outside the back door.

Of course I chased them! That's what I do!

And mom really should have known that I would chase them right into a grouping of several deer who had bedded down in the trees to wait out the imminent storm. Startled deer run. I didn't make them run. But of course I chased them. That's what I do!

I never told them to run right into a herd of the neighbor's cattle but you better believe that when they did, I followed right along. Because COWS.

Okay, so maybe I am somewhat to blame for getting too excited when I saw the cows and jumping that barbed wire fence into the neighbor's field, but how was I to know that the fencing would trap me in the field, away from the bunnies and deer and cows? If I had known that, I never would've jumped the fence!

Lucky for us the neighbor drove his truck down the road at just that moment, and I chased him along the road for nearly half a mile, all the way into our driveway and mom's open arms.

So now mom's punishing me by making me come inside early, but (shh, don't tell her) that's okay by me because I am exhausted from all that gallivanting around and am totally ready for a nap.

74

Mom woke me up after my bunny-deer-cow-truck racing. She said I'd been snoring on her couch for four hours and I should go outside for my nightly constitutional before going to bed, but I was too tired. I tried heading upstairs instead but I didn't make it very far before lying down again.

Okay, okay, don't laugh. I only made it to the second step. Seriously, you try chasing bunnies and deer and cows and trucks and see if you can make it up all ten steps to bed!

Luckily mom was able to lift all seventy pounds of me and carry me up to bed.

Yup, I am one loved pup. Today was just an awesome day … *snore.*

Good morning, world!

Boy do I feel totally refreshed. Mom says a sixteen hour "nap" will do that to a pup. So it's off to explore the big outside world again ... hey, wait a minute. Why is that very unhappy, overly dramatic squirrel telling me off? All I did was race out the back door!

I told mom that this would not end well.

One of those pesky woodpeckers just discovered one of the many hiding places the squirrels use to escape all the night-time monsters and evil predators. Of course the woodpecker is going to town on this hiding place, just banging his nose against it over and over and over and over and over.

It gives me a headache just thinking about it, so you know the squirrels must be in agony. So I told mom about it, but she just kind of shrugged and said there was nothing we could do.

Now the squirrels are organizing a lynch mob.

It's Birds vs. Squirrels.

Just between you and me, I'm rooting for the squirrels because I love their fluffy twitching tails (but don't tell the birds—I don't want them dive bombing me when I am out exploring the fields).

77

But mooooooommmmmm!

The deer ran, so I *had* to chase it! You can't blame me for following it. I didn't know it was heading for the creek down by the road.

By the way, that place is really cool—and so many new wildlife friends that I have never met before. Can I go swimming down there again tomorrow?

78

Okay, bunnies. I realize you want to play, and I am fine with that. I really am. But do you mind taking your game to someplace other that my picture window? I am on sentry duty today and you keep distracting me! Why do you torture me so?

Pistachio: Mom! Wake up! There's something outside. I can hear it in the trees. Can you hear it? Listen ... listen ... there it is! What's that noise? Is it aliens in invading? I will totally protect you. You stay in bed, and I will sit on your chest to protect you. Because that noise is close, so they're getting close, right? Don't worry. I'll put on my scary face. *Grrrr.*

Mom: Pistachio, it's four in the morning! Go back to sleep.

Pistachio: Don't worry, mom. I got this. I got you covered. Lily's got the floor protected, and I am protecting the bed. You're safe here. Promise—there it is again! That noise! *Grrr.*

Mom: That's a Great Horned Owl. He's just saying hi.

Pistachio: An owl? *Harrumph.* That's what they want you to think. The aliens, I mean. They want you to think you're all safe and snug in your bed, listening to the sounds of an owl, but really they're sneaking up on you. But they can't fool me. I got you covered. *Grrr.*

Lily: Shut up and go to sleep.

Pistachio: *Whimper.* Yes, ma'am.

...

Pistachio (quietly): *Grrr.*

We survived the aliens! The wildlife neighbors decided to celebrate by throwing a deer parade this morning right as mom took us out for our morning walks. I tried to join in the parade, but all the deer took off running for the trees.

Must have been a short parade.

But we survived the aliens!

Mom went out to get the mail. She didn't take me with her today, which made me sad.

Then I saw her talking to one of the deer, who stopped by to say hi.

So now I'm teaching mom a lesson by giving her the silent treatment.

I'm not sure she's noticed yet.

This may not have been the most well-thought-out plan.

82

The only thing scarier than aliens invading at four in the morning is Baby getting into mom's recent batch of catnip that she harvested.

Excuse me as I just go over here to hide behind mom until Baby's eyes go back to normal.

83

When mom brought me home to live with her, she already had Lily, who was probably fifteen years old when I arrived. Lily is a master floor cleaner. No matter what drops (crumbs, mom's pen, the ball from my mouth), she is there to swoop in and eat it (or attempt to). She uses this skill outside as well, which disturbs mom quite a bit because Lily is always grabbing up stuff that even I wouldn't roll in (must less eat). And once she has something, she does not let go (despite missing one of her canines). She may have a lot of white around the face, but she never acts as old as she is (unless you wake her up when she's sleeping, and then she's ancient!)

But Lily is also losing her hearing, and sometimes she misses a dropped item. Like this morning, when mom accidentally dropped a piece of bread from her toast right next to Lily's leg. Lily was sleeping and didn't realize that food was nearby. So I quietly crept over to the crumb and picked it up before tiptoeing back to my kennel to munch on it, also as quietly as possible.

I still can't believe I got away with it.

84

Several deer just meandered past the bedroom window, with one even stopping to look in at me.

Naturally I barked. Naturally I lunged. Naturally the window shattered.

How is any of this my fault? It's just nature.

85

Sometimes mom has the strangest reactions to things. Take today, for instance. We were all in the kitchen, just hanging out and watching mom put stuff away in the cupboards, when a full box of doggie treats slipped from her grasp and fell between me and Lily.

We saw this event as reason to celebrate.

Mom shrieked as if aliens were taking over her body.

Sometimes humans are just too strange.

Squirrels vs. Birds continues ...

I was sitting sentry at the picture window when I saw a squirrel scamper up the back of mom's car. Naturally, I issued a soft whine to warn mom. When that didn't work, I barked once. I thought the squirrel might be trying to steal mom's car and she needed to know, right?

Mom came over to look out the window with me. She said the squirrel has found a new nest area in the spare attached to the back of her car. She didn't seem too worried, but I stayed vigilant.

Then the barn swallows started diving and attacking the squirrel as he popped his head in and out of the spare tire area.

I started to bark, but then I wondered: Who am I barking at? The squirrel for being a squirrel? Or the birds who were harassing my squirrel friend?

Philosophical questions make my head hurt, so I just sat at my sentry post, issuing a mutated growl-whimper-bark-whine while the squirrel popped his head in and out and the barn swallows dove and attacked. Mom said it was like a surreal whack-a-mole game.

Mom got me the coolest present: a new pool.

Okay, so I had a pool before this, and it was really big, so I could stretch out and roll around in the water. But I guess I got a little too excited with it a few times, jumping in and out and back in again, and I cracked the bottom so it wouldn't hold water anymore. I was really sad.

But mom loves me because she got me a new, stronger pool, and she already set it up. I was so excited for it to fill up with water so I could zoom around the acreage over and over and then collapse in the pool to cool off. Then mom told me I had to wait, and I was so sad.

I sat by the window, staring out at my new pool friend, and that's when mom pointed out why I had to wait: The butterflies and birds and squirrel and bunnies and even the deer were all enjoying *my* pool! I counted fourteen birds (orioles, robins, a blue jay, and others) taking turns while six butterflies flitted in and out of the water. The squirrels would sneak in when they could, and one mama bunny found a way to get some water from the back side of the pool. A bunch of birds were in the tree above the pool, and two deer stood by the tree as well, all waiting their turn. Meanwhile, one robin was having a private bath in my water dish!

So I am trying to sit calmly and quietly so my friends can drink from the cool water, but I can't wait to get out there and chase them, zooming all over!

88

These silly cats. All three have been stalking a little mouse for the last two days. Mom tried to trap it in the bathroom, but it got out and ran right by all three sleeping cats.

Luckily I saw it and grabbed it up so I could take it to mom. She likes to let the mice go live outside (lucky mice!).

I still don't understand why mom screamed so loud when I dropped the little mouse in her bed.

The birdie living in the nest above the front door has babies! Lots of little babies in one teeny tiny nest. Mama birdie lets mom and Lily go on the porch, but when I try to go out there, she attacks me, so now I have to hide between mom's legs. The poor delivery guy had it even worse, because the mama birdie chased him all the way back to his truck! How can something so small be so terrifying?

90

Pistachio: What foul beast has taken to sleeping in my bed? And with my favorite ball clasped in her front paws? No! NO! I will have none of this! Awake, heathen! Be gone from my bed!

Mom: Hush, P-dawg.

Pistachio: The horror! The travesty! I will not stand for it!

Mom: Give me a break. Lily can't hear you anyway.

Pistachio: Fine. But if she gets to sleep in my bed, then I get to sit on your lap, right?

91

Today I got to meet Mr. Toad, who has burrowed into the soft dirt in the middle of all of mom's vegetables.

Of course, when I tried to enjoy that cool, soft dirt, mom yelled at me. Apparently toads are special. I don't understand why. I tried to say hi to him, but he just made me gag and start frothing at the mouth.

Mom and Lily laughed at me.

I think I will just leave him be. For now.

Tonight's pre-bedtime constitutional was a bit ... awkward. Mom took out outside on leash so we could do our business. I had just let loose when I noticed a deer standing next to the trees, not twenty feet away from us.

Of course, I really wanted to run and play with the deer, who had obviously stopped by for a visit, but, *ahem*, I was mid stream and couldn't really stop. So I continued about my business, hoping the new friend would understand the delay.

Just as I was finishing up, there was a noise in the weeds and we all—deer, mom, me—turned to see what could be making so much racket. (Only Lily didn't seem bothered by the noise, but then again, she probably didn't hear any of it.) We all stared at the weeds, waiting for something truly ginormous (and undoubtedly evil) to emerge.

But whatever was in there apparently decided that three on one were not odds in its favor, so the noise suddenly stopped (which, in truth, was even creepier than the noise was). The deer took this as a sign and lifted its back leg slowly before suddenly pivoting and dashing off into the trees. I made a similar move, dragging mom and Lily back into the house.

Tonight, I must be vigilant in standing guard to protect mom and ... *snore*.

A fly has decided to play tag with me.
Game on, little pest.
I pounce, duck left and right, then go in for the kill and *bam* run head-first into the wall.

The fly is winning. The cats are laughing.

Sometimes life is so unfair.

Mom's been really frustrated lately because something has been eating her lettuce, beets, and carrot tops. Personally, I think it's Mr. Toad, because he keeps getting fatter and fatter, but mom says even Mr. Toad can't eat all that food.

Today, we found out who the culprit really is.

I was standing at the back door, waiting to go outside. Mom was watching the birds, who were all hanging out in the tree above the pool. She said that they were afraid of me, which is why they weren't in the pool.

Just to be clear, there really is no need to be afraid of me. I am happy to share my pool and puppy kisses with anyone.

Okay, fine, except Mr. Toad.

Anyway, back to the door and going outside. Mom finally opens the door and I lunge outside and trip on a dark greyish cat. Aha! See? The birds are not afraid of me!

Except it wasn't a cat. It was a woodchuck, which makes more sense because cats don't eat vegetables from the garden. We watched it run to a tree, which it climbed in a scampering sort of way. He got maybe two feet up (we never moved the whole time because we were just staring at him), then decided to go back down the tree and hide at the base of it in the grass.

Mom giggled at that point, which is probably what sent him to the wood pile next. He paused, reassessed, then ran to the garage. Pause. Around the corner. Pause. Through the grass to the big tree outside the dog run. Pause. Back into the weeds.

I lost him after that, and mom wouldn't let me off leash the rest of the day. But I promise I will find my cute new friend again someday and make the proper introductions.

95

Baby and I were sitting in the front window, enjoying then sun, when a red-headed woodpecker arrived at the watering hole (*ahem*, my pool). I think this woodpecker must have beat his head one too many times because he started telling off a group of robins that were enjoying their morning bath.

I don't know about you, but if it ever becomes woodpeckers vs. robins, I am betting on the robins. They may not be the feistiest of birds, but they have numbers on their side.

96

It was too hot to do any exploring today, so I decided to just hang out inside.

I thought about trying to start a game with mom. I sat up, looked at mom, and picked up my toy, but then I yawned, dropped my toy, shook my head, turned in two circles, and plopped back down—right on top of my toy.

Today was definitely a nap-all-day day. Maybe we can play tomorrow ...

Mr. Toad came back today. Naturally. I found him bedded down in a freshly planted row of fall crops. But I think he may have moved on from vegetables and now is eating rabbits because he is huge!

He started a stare down with me. Yeah, Mr. Toad totally won. He even gave me a derisive snort (well, a face that said "I would send you off with a derisive snort if I could make such a noise").

I kinda wish the woodchuck would come back and scare Mr. Toad off again.

98

Why is it that the aliens always try to attack in the middle of the night?

Last night I discovered three new types of aliens on the front porch. They looked like big fat squirrels only with darker fur. Mom said they were raccoons. Whatever they were, they were trying to come in the front door, so I barked as loudly as I could to send them on their way.

Seriously, it's just polite to drop in unexpectedly when everyone is sleeping!

Two of the scoundrels ran for cover in the cornfield but the third decided to climb a nearby tree ... the tree whose branches come close to the bedroom window. I'm not so sure these wannabe squirrels are too smart because if mom would've opened the window, I could've reached out and nabbed that raccoon.

99

Charlie was sitting in the window, just hanging out as usual, when he suddenly started "talking" to something outside, in a friendly "how do" neighborly meow. Then he stretched up to the top of the window, still friendly as all get out. When I looked up at what got him so excited, fully expecting to see a bird or a butterfly, I saw a squirrel!

Wait a minute! I thought the squirrels were *my* friends!

This squirrel was peering down at Charlie, not even three inches from the window. When the squirrel saw me, she took off, but she has been racing back and forth in front of the window for the last ten minutes, swishing her tail all around.

Now she is sitting under the window and staring up at Charlie. Uh, I think the squirrel has a crush on Charlie.

100

Apparently the raccoons have returned with reinforcements: a trio of coyotes. They are sitting under the bedroom window and serenading me. Of course I joined in on the howl-fest. I couldn't be rude!

While running around to explore the acreage this morning, I found something hiding in an old pipe lodged between a log and the fence. I am pretty sure it was a mouse, so I wanted to nab it and bring it back to mom. But first I had to get the mouse.

Unfortunately, I couldn't fit my face into the greasy pipe, so I decided to snuggle down between the pipe and the log and wait for my new friend to come out and play.

When mom found me a while later, she laughed and laughed. Apparently I got a whole bunch of new (grease) spots all over my face.

Of course, I didn't find it as funny because mom decided I had to have a bath before I could go inside and eat dinner. I don't understand why she is always so worried about me being clean. I'm just going to get dirty again tomorrow.

ABOUT THE AUTHOR

Dog wrangler, cat slave, turkey observer, cow racer, raccoon enabler ... these are just a few of the jobs that keep Nanette M. Day busy on her acreage. When she's not watching Mother Nature's songbirds, quadrupeds, and creepy crawlies, Nanette writes books detailing their shenanigans.

In addition to writing humorous vignettes of how her furries are taking over the world (one nap at a time), she writes gritty flash fiction and short stories as well as small-town romance novels.

Puppy Kisses Book 2

In the next installment of Puppy Kisses, you will go on an adventure with Pistachio, where you get to decide which paths to take. Will you end up running with the deer or staring down the monster in the trees?

~

Puppy Kisses Book 3

The adventures continue...

Puppy Kisses
Book 3

life as a dog in the
COUNTRY

ADDITIONAL WORKS WRITTEN AS C. JAI FERRY

Skeleton Dance

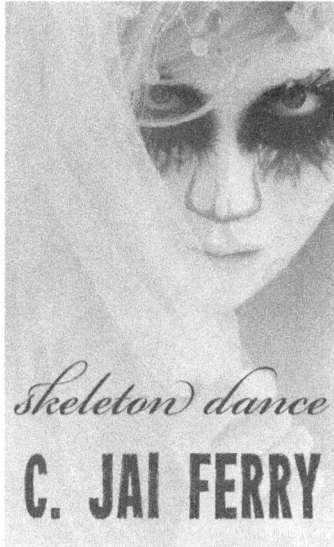

"My grandmother wanted to kill me..."

So begins a dark and disturbing look into a world that is all too real for thousands of children every day. "Skeleton Dance" is the story of one young girl's perseverance in surviving the eccentricities of her grandmother. Despite being harassed in a multitude of ways, this young girl is able to stand up to her grandmother in both small and grandiose ways. Sometimes victorious, but more often not, she ultimately grows into a woman faced with the biggest challenge yet: Follow the well-worn path of the matriarchs in her family or strike out into virgin territory.

Unraveled

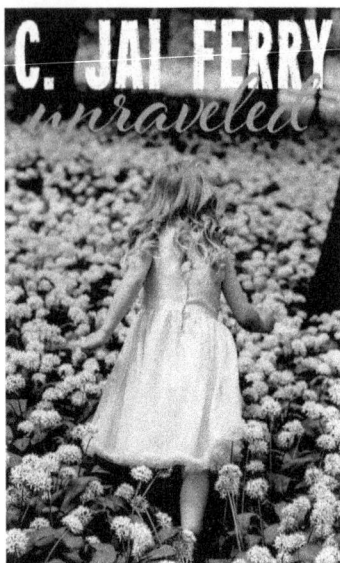

Step into a world of struggling fathers, aging English teachers, terrified mothers, plague-bearers, revenge artists, ill-fated lovers, and children searching for their place in life—all characters brought to life in the flash fiction of C. Jai Ferry. Ferry uses evocative language and imagery to highlight those telling moments when a person's entire life changes from a seemingly simple decision. These bite-sized morsels, most fewer than 100 words, examine the human condition and all its bittersweet moments.

ADDITIONAL WORKS WRITTEN AS
CORRISSA JAMES

Great Plains Romance series

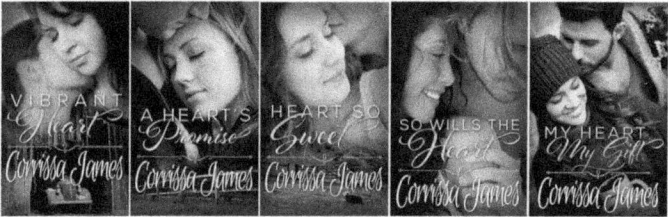

Small-town romance never looked so good. The entire series is available now.